TOOLS FOR TEACHERS

- **ATOS:** 0.8
- **GRL:** C
- **WORD COUNT:** 58

- **CURRICULUM CONNECTIONS:** animals, habitats

Skills to Teach

- **HIGH-FREQUENCY WORDS:** here, in, on, run, the, they, we, who
- **CONTENT WORDS:** badgers, bison, dens, grass, hawks, prairie, pronghorn, rest, sky, snakes, sun, visit
- **PUNCTUATION:** periods, question marks, apostrophe, exclamation point
- **WORD STUDY:** r-controlled vowels (*prairie, pronghorn, soar*); /ng/ (*pronghorn*); long /i/, spelled *i* (*bison*), *y* (*sky*); short /u/, spelled *u* (*sun*), *o* (*bison*); /j/, spelled *dg* (*badgers*)
- **TEXT TYPE:** information report

Before Reading Activities

- Read the title and give a simple statement of the main idea.
- Have students "walk" though the book and talk about what they see in the pictures.
- Introduce new vocabulary by having students predict the first letter and locate the word in the text.
- Discuss any unfamiliar concepts that are in the text.

After Reading Activities

Ask the children to think about the environment that is the focus of the book. What do they think a prairie is like? Invite them to discuss what makes a prairie and then to name other animals and plants they think might live there.

Tadpole Books are published by Jump!, 5357 Penn Avenue South, Minneapolis, MN 55419, www.jumplibrary.com

Copyright ©2018 Jump. International copyright reserved in all countries. No part of this book may be reproduced in any form without written permission from the publisher.

Editorial: Hundred Acre Words, LLC   **Designer:** Anna Peterson

Photo Credits: Adobe Stock: hkuchera, 8–9; Martha Marks, 2–3. Dreamstime: Sermovik, 14–15. Getty: Danita Delimont, 12–13. Shutterstock: irin-k, 1; Jason Patrick Ross, 6–7; Keneva Photography, 12–13; missanzi, cover; Steve Cukrov, 4–5.

Library of Congress Cataloging-in-Publication Data
Names: VanVoorst, Jenny Fretland, 1972– author.
Title: Who lives on the prairie? / by Jenny Fretland VanVoorst.
Description: Minneapolis, Minnesota: Jump!, Inc., (2017) | Series: Who lives here? | Audience: Age 3–6. | Includes index.
Identifiers: LCCN 2017032056 (print) | LCCN 2017034482 (ebook) | ISBN 9781624967290 (ebook) | ISBN 9781620319611 (hardcover: alk. paper) | ISBN 9781620319628 (pbk.)
Subjects: LCSH: Prairie animals—Juvenile literature.
Classification: LCC QL115.3 (ebook) | LCC QL115.3 .V36 2017 (print) | DDC 591.74—dc23
LC record available at https://lccn.loc.gov/2017032056

WHO LIVES ON THE PRAIRIE?

by Jenny Fretland VanVoorst

TABLE OF CONTENTS

tadpole
books

WHO LIVES ON THE PRAIRIE?

Let's visit the prairie.

Who lives here?

bison

Bison live here.

They feed on the grass.

Snakes live here.

They lie in the sun.

Badgers live here.

They rest in their dens.

Hawks live here.

They soar in the sky.

Pronghorn live here.

pronghorn

They run in the grass.

Who else lives here?

We do!

WORDS TO KNOW

badgers

bison

hawks

prairie

pronghorn

snakes

INDEX

16